The Distant Hills

Poems by

I. G. Buenaseda

To Stella,

Best Wishes!

Sincerely
I. g. buenaseda
11/22/02

ISBN: 1-4033-2847-1 (Electronic)
ISBN: 1-4033-2848-X (Softcover)

This book is printed on acid free paper.

1stBooks - rev. 06/03/02

Contents

Attempts

My pen is a walking cane
tapping its way on the blank sheet.
Each tap is an appropriate word,
each word a determined step
in the tricky mountain paths
carefully chosen to note down
the long struggle of my people.

My pen shall find its way
to the bosoms of the masses
to write their songs and their longings
articulate their hopes and misfortunes,
awaken their sentiments,
enhance the creative power within them
and be with them in their liberation.

Morning Poem

Darkness seeps in heavily
like a black mist upon this room.
It is three o'clock in the morning
what a strange hour to wake up
when the whole world is asleep.
Like the darkness,
elemental questions prick the mind
sending ripples of thoughts
in search of meanings.

Five o'clock in the morning
is the familiar sound of someone
moving in the kitchen.
Nobody greets the dawn
in the city anymore.
Only the cars
herald the birth of a new day.

At eight o'clock in the morning
the man ambles down the street,
spreads his arms and offers himself
for the world to possess.

The Ricebirds are Back in San Roque

In August, when the green sea
turns golden in the sunlight,
I shall be home in San Roque
and listen to the songs
of the returning ricebirds.
The hiss of the rice stalks
when the breeze passes by
are the sound of the thousand blades
that liberated our people
from poverty and oppression.
The ricebirds will sing once more
the names of those who struggled
silently in the shadows.
The peasants remember them
on the night of blades and bullets
that destroyed the fetters
after years of fear and silence.
Today, San Roque
is alive once more.

An Evening at the Landlord's Mansion

Where were you
when we ransacked the hacienda,
when waves of brown bodies
shattered the iron gate
that defined the limits of relation?
We were there with torches and blades.
Eyes that used to stare blankly
were ablaze with passion.
You should have seen the landlord
and his untouchable clan
cowered in the perfumed room
clutching helpless crucifixes.
You should have seen their eyes
glazed like those of cornered rats
reflecting the terror deeper than death,
that fundamental fear
made more horrifying with the awareness
of their doom in the hands of the peasants.
They were no longer arrogant
strange for these people
who institutionalized violence
would tremble at the sight of blood and fire.
You should have been there.
The young women whose supple bodies
warmed the landlord's bed
and appeased his loin,

those who were ordered around
to make the daily lives of the landlord
and his clan easy and comfortable
were all there surrounding the master
who could no longer insult,
threaten and brutalize the simple folks.

Ayala, 5:30 p.m.

The last click clack of the keyboards
are drumbeats that send shuffling feet
down the automatic staircase
where people look at each other
and see shrunken images of defeated souls.
Outside, after five o'clock,
the streets greet the swelling crowd
that pop up like puppets
liberated from the constricting embrace
of deadlines and imperatives.
The high heeled shoes lick the pavement
as streams of mobile faces
exhale the accumulated tumult,
tension and discontent.
In the sputtering sunlight
men in briefcases talk of devaluation,
labor unrest and foreign loans
as they keep track of the areas
where the peasants opted to hold guns
instead of the plows.
Dirty street children
chant the canticle of the exploited crowd
while the traffic lights
blinks with indifference.

Tonight, the street sweepers
shall brush away the day's refuse
as the descending darkness
tuck in the paranoia and delusions
of those who rule.
But tomorrow, Ayala Avenue will be
clean again.

Balangiga Revisited

The ricebirds have returned to Balangiga
to sing the legend of a people
of the men and women
who survived the howling wilderness
and defied the grandiose dream
of an empire built on the blood and tears
of the red, black, brown and yellow races.
Their cries still reverberate
on the conscience of a nation
despite the computerized efforts
to cover up the atrocities
with Mickey Mouse education.
The flames that consumed their homes
flicker in the eyes of the younger generation
who are carrying on the struggle
and call back to life the resolute fight
of those who died in this honored Samar town.
They will always remember
that dawn in Balangiga
when whispered notes and silent nods
signaled death and liberation.

Tacloban City

In this city
where the streets lead to the sea
you'll feel the youthful urgency
of a modern metropolis
about to be born.
Its pavements echo the footsteps
of men in search of a dream.
Expectation is written
On the faces in the crowd
you meet in the sidewalks
in wharves, in marketplaces.
It won't be long
before its familiar landmarks
would only be monuments
of another age.
On their places will rise modern industries.
Rise up, lovely city
take your steps with confidence
among the cities of the world,
drain your swamplands
turn them into golden fields of grains
cultivate your seas, level your hills
bring to the countryside
and among your slums
new technology for your people.
Are not the benefits of science
the common heritage of mankind?
Absorb the warmth of the eastern sun
It is not only the leaves and the birds
that greet the dawn each day

but the toiling men
and those who shall inherit this earth.
Let the murmur of the sea
mingle with the whir of engines
into a symphony of progress.
In a young and determined city
all is possible.

To an Emerging Metropolis

Fingers of steel stretch upward
and puncture the skyline.
These are the patterns
from which the city evolves
molded by the hands of the workers
whose labor shapes civilizations.

O my city
build your towers
gild them with rainbows and gold
and reach for the heavens.
Drain your steaming marshes
and in its place
put up a man-made paradise.
Open your arms to foreign friends
show them the untarnished
beauty of your land.

But look down, my city,
from your skyscrapers
among the shanties that border
your industrial centers
the simple villages that fringe your shores.
Look down on your people
breed in ignorance and poverty
for what use is the splendor of a city
when the countrysides
seethe with discontent.

Gandara River

Drip by drip the sweat of the earth
coalesced in some secluded bowels
deep in the heartland of Samar.
Prompted by the forces of nature
to surge in the warmth of sunlight
and send unending messages
from scattered settlements
to the cities of the world.
Now silent, slow and deep
then rushing down
among rocks and valleys
in light and shadows, always onward.
No amount of repression
can check your course
Oh, mighty river
like the formidable people
united in struggle
against oppression and tyranny
gathering strength along the way
wave upon wave in turbulent expurgation
to flood the earth, destroy and recreate.

Sohoton Cave

Nature's cathedral
hewn from the original rocks
where jewel-encrusted spires
dripping through the ages
betray earth's painful metamorphosis.
Immortal cave of many tales
neither the playful sunbeams
nor the cold stares of distant stars
disturb the sacred silence of primal darkness.
This impenetrable void wakes up the senses,
provokes the mind
to the romantic and the mysterious.
Are these the lore
your splendid chambers keep?
The aggregate knowledge of generations
extant among the unlettered folks
who come to worship in your awesome dome.
What danger lurks in the unknown
tranquil waters oozing from your bowels
to the violence of the open sea?
Ah, magnificent cave!
Men have for ages scaled your depth
each in search for answers
to timeless interrogations,
to feel the endless rhythm of the universe.

I. G. Buenaseda

It is not only the sun and the sea
that endure the test of time
but the quiet dignity of your beauty
revealed only to brave souls
who ventured to go deeper
into the primal darkness of your heart.

Maqueda Bay

Quivering sunrays filtered through liquid jade
which renders purer lights
in the twilight world of water creatures
moving in perfect grace
dreamlike among purple corals
while far beneath the obscure depths
breathe the unspeakable fecundity of ocean life.
In this silent world of refracted images
the mortal eyes, unaccustomed
to the solemn stillness of the deep
can only see at arm-length
guided by phosphorescent traces of rippling lines
to sink farther into the darkened chambers
of the sea and feel the cold embrace
of unmoving waters.

Zumarraga

Cradled in the ancient island of Buad
in the heart of Samar Sea
where seabirds build the homes
among the rocks and in the marshland
nestles the island town of Zumarraga.

Here, the world is circumscribed
by the rhythm of the tides
and happiness is hidden
in the pristine waters
of some secluded beaches
far from the stress and tensions
of the world.

The night comes softly
like the music of a distant guitar
as one by one the seabirds
return to their nests among the marshes
in an endless ritual of homecoming.

What futile dreams do men pursue
searching for heaven
in mirrored rooms and violet lights
framed in flashy boulevards
amid the screams and clamor
of a bustling metropolis.

That piece of paradise
is found in the humble lives
of simple folks,
in little songs that go deep
into the soul.
How can one say goodbye to Zumarraga
when like clusters of memories
it is always in the mind.

To a Political Detainee

The prison bars
have isolated you
from the masses you love so much.
The tyrant's men
thinking that mortal pain
would force you to betray
the masses are baffled.
In their simple mindedness
they failed to understand
why you stand firm and resolute
even in unbearable torture.
They would not know
that you've found the meaning
of selfless love
in the service of the people
They arrested you in the vain hope
that brutality and indignities
would crush your spirit
and hold back, even for a moment,
their inevitable doom.
Within your prison walls
you will hear the rumbling
of angry voices,
the fury of an awakened nation.
You will feel the violent surge
of the people's armed resistance
wave upon wave, from victory to victory.

The people whom you served
so selflessly are coming
to tear away your prison walls
and together assume
a fresh and higher task.

I. G. Buenaseda

Basilio

It might have been quite difficult
to shield yourself from the insistence of memory.
Each night is a bout with images popping in the mind
flaying the soul to keep the impressions alive
lest you forget the outrage and the shame.
You should have felt the master's unerring whip
cut rivulets of blood in yours mother's naked back.
You've heard her screams of pain
the unworded agony of our people
echoing through the centuries.
In your pained recollection
you saw Juli and the pristine woodland
where you sought refuge
on the night of death and madness.
How you chilled your blood to summon numbness
for the humiliation of your trampled manhood.
And now you immersed yourself
in books hoping to change the world
that you would not retrace the footsteps
of your forebears
so you can watch with apathy
the infernal fear sprawl on their faces
even as they were consoled
with the promise of paradise.
How you endured the whims of your masters
in their frizzled world of empty gestures
so you can join their exotic circle
and eventually be one of them,
looking down at your benighted people
hearing their cries and fearing their wrath!

You've missed the point, Basilio,
faithful to the class that you serve
and aspire to be a part, you look pathetic
in that fateful hour when you let history slipped
through your fingers in a gesture of ignominy.

I. G. Buenaseda

To a Renegade Priest

You will not seek the hangman's tree
as your predecessor did
at least he sought to assuage his conscience
from the jingles of silver.
With you it is different
despite the habit
you have not fully understood
the gospel of national liberation
which makes you even more loathsome
for the betrayal of the people
was more conscious and deliberate.
Poor and simple men are made of better stuff
the unlettered peasants
who constitute your flock
have withstood the realities of violence
their gentle bodies yielding
to the sharpness of steel
and if you think your confession
would check the revolutionary surge
sweeping the countrysides
you are completely wrong.
Collaboration will not silence those
who have gone deeper into the struggle.
You will surely outlive most of them
as they meet death with dignity
while you cling to life in shame.

History has placed them
in the bosoms of the people
while you and your kind
have only the legacy of compromise
dangling between your legs.

Dewdrops for my Lady

1

My eyes are heavy
but I must tarry yet
before the moon is up.

2

I raise my glass to the stars
and ask the night
will she ever come?

3

Who cares, replied the night,
the wine is fragrant
with memories.

4

Is that her footsteps I hear?
Oh, it is only the rustling
of the leaves.

5

Drink some more, said the night,
your mind is dimmed
with sorrow.

6

My hands are cold with dews
but the wine gets warmer
with every sip.

Between Bottles of Beer

In this lonely room
I fashion you
from flimsy images
rippling in my mind.
One does not see faces
in a glass of beer
there is only sadness
in every sip.

The music from the old records
lingers in this room
my bed, empty and wide,
remembers the fragrance
of your hair.

Tomorrow,
you shall see me battered
like a wounded bird
upon this bed
but tonight
the hours are just right
for squeezing loneliness
between beer bottles.

I. G. Buenaseda

Into the Mirror of Our Eyes

Here is where we stand
face to face in this room
where we lit candles at midnight
searching for our discarded souls
in books written by strange men
in a medium we communicate
and conjure images.

The books are crowding in the shelves ·
faithless and alienated tools
by which we shape our minds
and cling to our misguided hopes.
We never cease to wonder
why we aspire for something
we are not.

In this familiar room
we listen to half-remembered voices
speaking in the language of our people.
Pick up the candle
and let us look once more
into the mirror of our eyes
retrace the silent agony of our spirits
struggling to be born.

Touch Me With Your Love

If I summon some dewdrops
to soothe your wounded heart
and pull back the hours
to allay the anguish
my reckless tongue
have caused you so much pain
then I shall come to you
in soft lingering whispers
as the breeze would
upon your window panes
to chant the guilt
within my heart
and kiss your watered eyes
and if by chance
I shall be a part of your dreams
like a single note in a concert
of broken ripples
then touch me
with the tendrils of your love
even with the slightest
breathe of sympathy
suffuse me with tenderness
as the moonlight would
a multitude of hopes.

I. G. Buenaseda

Night Song

Nobody notices the moon
suspended in the city skyline
like a forgotten lantern.
Far below, in the streets,
the moonlight quietly cuts
shinny ribbons of soft beams
caressing darkened alleyways.

The homeless have settled
in the sidewalks
embracing empty bottles
which are their private world.
Why do the streets
look so sad after the rain?

The music still echoes
in the empty corridors
while weary footsteps
lead to familiar doors
but I must linger yet
and in the silent moonlight
shape my thoughts
before the night takes flight.

Janet's 50th Summer

The season of cold twilight is over
and the lovers who populate
your morning dreams are gone.
Only the strains of half remembered songs
resound in the stale air of your room.

Strange men savored
the warmth of your early years
when your supple body
satiated their nocturnal quest
for the exotic and the forbidden,
when gaiety seemed an endless fountain
burbling in the violet lights of your room.

But time has snatched away
your pleasant dreams.
Your nimble feet can dance no more
and your lovely voice
is now the sound of a broken guitar.
Come now, Janet,
let us walk the familiar corridors
where your circular glories faded
with your dreams.

I. G. Buenaseda

Barok
(a mixed breed, 75% Duberman)

Those who have known you
must have wondered
why we shower you with affection
much like the way we love our friends.
They say that dogs like you
should know better where to stay
on the lowly place consigned
to animals like ducks and pigs.
Yet, we found in you that simple
kind of devotion, free from the whims
and selfishness that encumber human love,
that faith which extends beyond
the level of day to day relations
moved only by a primitive attachment
to someone who cares.
You've shown it more eloquently
than so many words, more meaningful
than the touch of human hands.

The Homeless

The old man on the
corner of 5th and Broadway
is a permanent fixture
of the daily street scene.
His breast is a cavern
of the deepest sorrow
and in his gaze
the silent indifference
of the world.
With sadness in his eyes
he reaches toward the crowd
for a little measure of sympathy.
But the city is cold and insensitive
to those who can not cope
with its imperatives.
Clutching a beer bottle
he ambles down the back streets
among the refuse of the city
away from the crowd
towards nevermore.

I. G. Buenaseda

Storming the Gates of Malacanang

All of us were there
from all places we came
familiar faces, chanting
with the rhythmic undulation
of the crowd, brown waves
flowing towards the gate.

First the youth and the students,
the sons and daughters of our land
resolute with their placards and slogans.
Then those who came from the fields,
the peasants, hard and determined
as they left untended rows
of paddies and green hills.
The workers were everywhere
the vendors too, and many more.
Their gaze intent in the gathering dusk.

We came not just for the sake of being there
the workers had come
with a catalogue of discontent
those who work the fields
because the politicians grabbed their lands.
The mothers came too
looking for their sons
who disappeared without a trace
There were no tears in their eyes
only pain and sufferings.

The gate loomed dark
upon the restless crowd
Nobody asked if we have the strength
the people are always strong
and no gate is impregnable
before the multitude.

the peasants, the ones who left their fields,
the wage earners and the young ones
the students and the youth
seized a fire truck
and rammed the iron gate
of the dictatorship
burned the cars inside
symbols of extravagance and greed.
They massed before the shattered gate
their heads bloody but determined.
Shaking their fists in defiance
they left and walked on
not back to their villages and fields
of paddies and young canes
nor among the sweatshops
and back alleys of the cities
but toward the distant hills:
to the heartland of the Cordilleras
forests of the Sierra Madre,
the islands of the Visayas
and the jungles of Mindanao.

I. G. Buenaseda

It's Time to Go

I have to go and leave you now
cross the river and not look back
lest I see the pain in your eyes.
I shall go beyond those hills
across the savannah
where we could move like shadows
among our people.

I shall be with you always
as you work on the field after the rain
or in the dried riverbed in summertime.
You will feel my presence
in the intimate touch of sunlight
my voice shall comfort you
in the nocturnal concerts of the winds.
You shall find me among the shades
blending with the rocks and foliage
or motionless among the ruins.
I shall come to you with the monsoon
and the gentle caress of summer.

The time has come for me to go
I have freed myself from doubts
and the meaningless interrogations.
I have to leave you now, my love,
so our children will have peace.

The Fisherman

He dips his paddle gently into the water
the way his hand caresses a woman's hair
and silently propels the boat
to some familiar spots, favorite corners
out where the fish congregate
among the purple corals of the reef.

He knows the sea so well
a deep intimacy to its moods and movements.
His hands can trace the contour of the waves
pull them tight, gather the breeze
and grasp the mystic potency of the tides.

Twilight brings him back to shore
where anxious housewives wait
to keep the evening fire ablaze.
Tonight, he would retire upon his bed
to dream of the sea, the salty sea
and the impulsive throbbing of distant shores.

I. G. Buenaseda

Mat Weavers of Basey

What patterns do your fingers
trace in the mat you are weaving?
Blades of grass slithering
between fingers reflect
the checkered lives of your people
inured to hardship and sacrifice.
They worked quietly all day
their sickles cut rhythmic orbits
around the shadows of the reeds
as they heave and bend
beneath the lash of the midday sun.
The marshland breathes heavily
like an exhausted water buffalo
as driftwoods point naked fists skyward
like drowning men,
grabbing the air as they sink.
What pictures do you present
oh, beautiful weavers of Basey
wild ducks resting among water hyacinths
on their way to distant land
and the nocturnal scenes
when the mournful calls
of marsh birds serenade the moon
while the reeds in shallow riverbeds
swayed with the unrelenting breeze.
put all of these in your mat
lovely weavers, as you contemplate
your secret longings and pains.

Time

One does not play with time
it is not something you jingle
or cuddle in your sleep.
Time is a fragment of eternity
flowing endlessly
without beginning
without an end.
It does not stop nor pause
just goes on and on
a luminous line
in the vast emptiness
that goes on forever
and ever.
Every second, the present
transforms itself
into the irretrievable past
even as it races
into the future
which is always beyond reach.
Time engages man briefly
ephemeral moments
of ecstasy and pain
then leaves without a trace.
That is why
we have to seduce time
seize the explosive moments
before they lapse into nothingness.
And when the dust settles down
look for another moment to seize.

Seashell Gatherer

I found her footsteps on the sands
before the tides claims them.
She was up early each day
pushing the tides before the sun
creaks among the mountaintops.
She would search among the rocks
her trained fingers would find
cupped among the corals
seashells with the colors of sunshine.
At times she would raise herself
waist deep among the reefs
to gaze at the clusters of huts
misty in the early dawn
Halfway through the day
she would head for home
her basket full of shinning shells
for strangers who come
to take pictures of places
and things the natives never thought
important or attractive.
These people find ordinary shell
exotic and wonder for how long
these isolated islands can sustain
their innocence and peace.

Uncertain Times

There is no way of telling
what will happen next.
Everything is fluid
and people are restless
anticipating something
they really do not know.
We cannot look out far
only the present matters.
Do not ask where our friends
have gone or if they are
coming back.
The day is completed
before we can even think
of tomorrow.
Times like this
affections are more poignant
amid instability and despair,
life becomes more meaningful
in the presence of death.

I. G. Buenaseda

The Distant Hills

It was summertime
when the armed men came
like wild dogs in the silent dawn.
They kicked the frail doors
and dragged the old men out
the muzzles of their guns
jabbed at hollow ribcages.
They shouted profanities
made the men squat on the roadside
squat on their haunches
the way most peasants do.
"You are hiding rebels among you,"
the officer said, as he circled them
"where are the young men?"
he asked and waited for an answer.
The old men remained silent.
"If they are not here by twelve o'clock,
You will all be detained."
But no amount of threats
could make the peasants talk.
At noon, the old men were lined up
barefooted on the dry river bed.
With a serious look in their eyes,
so familiar with those who know
the secrets of the forests,
they gazed knowingly at the distant hills
where their sons and daughters had gone.

With Sadness in Her Eyes

His mother was in the field
checking the young watermelons
when he came by to say goodbye.
He expected her to cry
but there was only sadness in her eyes.
"I do not know how your father
would take it", she said,
"he wanted you to work the land
as he and your ancestors did
many years ago, hacking their way
among trees and creepers.
Blades and flames leveled this ragged land
nourished it with their sweat and blood."
But his gaze was far beyond the land.
Without a backward glance,
he walked towards the horizon
as his mother watch him disappeared
in the hazy distance
with sadness in her eyes.

I. G. Buenaseda

Nothing Has Changed

After you left
they picked up your father
and three other men along the estero.
Suspects, they said
of an armed robbery
somewhere in Alabang.
After three days
their bodies floated
among the fish corrals
of Laguna de Bay.
How can we explain
that nothing has changed
in our lives
after all these years
that you were gone.

The Slums is Also a Home

Estero Real
was once a community,
clusters of shanties
nestled on slimy riverbank,
an interlace of naked alleys
lively with the sound
of playing children.

Today, Estero Real
is an empty space
deserted and forlorn
in a city of ever changing skyline.
The fishball stands
where workers ease hunger
from bamboo sticks
are no longer there.
The tricycle drivers
who used to convey workers
at the break of day
no longer ply their routes.

The simple working folks
have settled somewhere else
since the corporations
sent the bulldozers
and pushed the shanties
beyond the ridge.

There are no memories
to give comforts
in moments of sadness.
Only snatches of familiar songs
linger, sending ripples of pain
to those who indulge in recollection.
Neither are there names to remember
for it is more convenient to forget.

The shapeless corporations
and those living in swanky villages
would not understand
that the slums is a home.

Those who resettled elsewhere
will surely survive
in the embrace of other slums
they are inured to the hardship
and violence of the city
and in their hearts
there will always be Estero Real
where they once lived.

Farewell

I had to leave in haste
not knowing exactly
when I could be back.
I did not like to go
but strange eyes watched
in the shadows
and heavy fists knocked
at door on unusual hours
when people are asleep.

There was no time to say good bye
no time to pack up things
But I will always have
the delicate memories
of friends and comrades
who were gone,
those still in the hills
and in torture chambers.
Evelyn, my comrade in early years
died fighting for the people
in the plains of Nueva Ecija
There was also the memory of Bobby
gunned down one afternoon
in his humble clinic
in a coastal Samar town.

I can no longer share
Enlightened moments
With the sugar cane cutters of Kananga
Nor among the fishermen of Daram
As they braved the waves;
Their ingenious songs enhanced
The persistence of nostalgia.

From across the seas
in loneliness and pain
I will sing your name.
My songs are little notes
that will bring laughter
to your children
who were crying when I left.

I am coming back someday
when the monsoon flood the plains
and the Cordilleras resound
with the victorious celebrations,
when people march triumphant
their streamers flying in the breeze.
I shall be home when the islands
rise triumphant over the seas.

The Darkened Forest

Evening oozes gently upon the forest
descending from the canopy of leaves,
spreading softly among the rocks
embracing moss-covered tree trunks.

Darkness carries distinct charms
not visible in the haze of day
keeps the senses more alert to sounds
unfamiliar to human ears
and to scents suspended
in the purest air.

The darkened forest is a school
where we learn to disappear
among the rocks,
to cross deep ravines
balancing on fallen tree trunks.
We are learning from comrades
who are familiar with the terrain
and the hidden resources of the forest.
They can pick up gentle rustles
and decode signals from monkeys
announcing the presence of strangers,
the distinct noise of approaching footsteps
even on soggy earth are easily perceived.
They could feel vibration in the air
the invisible waves audible
to those who stay alert
in the service of the people.

I. G. Buenaseda

The darkened forest is not asleep;
nocturnal creatures enliven the air
with howls and mating calls.
Yet, the most steady sound is the beating
of one's heart and the voices within
of those who spend the nights in the forest
so that in the morning they can lure
and ensnare the enemies upon its bosom.

The Women of San Sebastian

The story has been told
that when the helicopters
landed at San Sebastian
and disgorged the raiding teams,
They did not find the men they were after.
Instead, they faced a human barricade
blocking the only pathway to the village.
Forming the barricade were the women
of San Sebastian.

The raiding teams, used to fight
armed guerillas, were perplexed
to confront unarmed women,
brave and defiant.
"No more," the women said,
"you have taken most of our men
leaving widows and orphans.
You do not feel the anguish,
the pain of losing loved ones."
A mother came forward
confronted the teams
"My boy, Reynaldo,
disappeared months ago
we never see him again."
Another followed:

"My husband and his two cousins
were peacefully tending their fields
when armed men appeared suddenly
and forced them to get in their trucks.
My husband returned after many weeks
badly beaten and his spirit broken.
No words about his cousins."

The leader of the raiding teams
got a megaphone and addressed the crowed:
"Listen, people of San Sebastian,
go home right now
take whatever you can
including your animals
and go to the next village
five miles down the river.
Anybody, young or old,
found in this village
after noon today will be shot."

And still on moonlight nights
those who passed along
the charred village of San Sebastian
swore that they could hear voices
of women calling onto them
to remember those who died
manning the barricade
many years ago and to keep
the struggle going.

I Will Always Be With You

In the dark days of my absence
I often see you in my dreams
misty in the distance.
Remembrances do not come easily
glimpses of the past still evoke
unexpected pain and sadness.
But how can one soften a resolute heart
and appease the steady prompting
of memories?

Your faith is my only guide, the north star
that keeps the hope alive for my return
from this forced exile and wandering.
Let me be a draft of air
to float on the wind
glide over your lakes and streams
way beyond the sweeping swampland
over the great plains and hidden valleys
follow the mountain ranges
down to the lovely islands
strewn like shattered beads
in the vast and open sea.

I shall move unseen and unrestrained
among our people, in villages by the sea
and in the never ending alleyways of our cities.

I. G. Buenaseda

I shall walk gently in the primal embrace
of your extended beaches, the very bosom
that nurtured your obscured heroes
and sustains the present day martyrs
in torture chambers and on the hills

You shall surely feel my presence
in the rhythm of the ocean
in the shadows of the forests
in the depths of the valleys
among neglected hamlets
in steamy workplaces and in picket lines.
You shall surely feel my presence
in the cold stare of mothers
waiting for their sons
who disappeared
in the middle of the night.

And when the multitude
come marching down
from the countrysides
to surround the city
you will find me among them.

Welcome

Open your doors
and ring the bells
the red warriors on the hills
shall descend at dawn
their eyes shining
with thousand stars.

The halls are empty now.
Those who ruled
with arrogance and greed
had fled in panic.

Together, we shall rebuild
our ravaged land,
redeem our lakes and rivers
from decadence.
The plains shall resound
with the songs
of returning rice birds
The cornfields shall bloom
once more.
There shall be food
for all our children.
There will be singing
and rejoicing at the plaza
of every town and city.

I. G. Buenaseda

The Tavern

The tavern is empty now
this usually crowded room
looks strange in the early hours
when the drunkards and the lovers
have settled in their private worlds.
Tables and chairs are mesmerized
into silence, almost perfect and final.
Even the streetlamps sputtered
with the loneliness of the seagulls.

The pier extends a mile long
punctuated by the shimmering harbor lights
and the fishermen's boats bobbling
lazily in the dark uneven waters.
Waves hesitate on wooden posts
before humming their lullabies.

Is it the outline of canoes
and the silent rhythm of the paddles
that appear and reappear
against the pale light of dawn?
Those who have gone to the other islands
are coming to the empty tavern
to meet with those who work
like shadows in this capital town.

The Battle of Mendiola Bridge
(January 30, 1970)

After the rain of rocks
and the staccato of machine guns
there was silence at Mendiola Bridge.
Four young men lay dead
fair sons of our native land
whose blood had sanctified
the bridge that set the boundaries
between the dictatorship and the people.

There was no turning back.
The baptism of blood and fire
had consolidated the youth
and made the bridge a memorial
to their commitment and sacrifice.

Bookbags are emptied
and refilled with the steady
supplies of rocks and bottles.
Up front, the youth battled
the soldiers and the police
bare fists and wooden clubs
against guns and the blinding mist
of tear gas.

Where did these young men and women
get the courage to defy truncheons and bullets?
It is the steadfast awareness that although
bullets can shatter their tender bodies
they can not destroy their commitment
to fight anything unjust and inhuman.

Where did they get the strength and endurance
to sustain their youthful energy
in a series of advances and retreats
amidst barbed wire and gunfires?
It came from the unqualified support
of the people in darkened alleyways
from rooftops, shops and homes
along Recto, Legarda and Aguila.
Through the extended night
pungent with tear gas and gun smoke
youth and students found safe havens
in the wide open doors
and warm embrace of the people.

It was a long an bloody night
pregnant with revolutionary impulses
to signal the start
of the first quarter storm
that would reverberate
in the countrysides.

At dawn, the youth honored
their martyrs with a new resolve
to continue the struggle in all fronts
in the service of the people.
And in their hearts
Mendiola Bridge had been enshrined
as a symbol of enlightened defiance
against the dictatorship.

I. G. Buenaseda

City Dreams

The family of Rufo and Myrna
with their three daughters
left the fishing village of Pandan
some years ago
in search of better life
in the city of many promises.

The sea had exhausted
its' resources
overfishing, the papers said.
Only the mayor
and his trawlers
went on fishing.

The city beckoned bright
with prospects and dreams.
There were always things to do
in the city, they said.
Money was easy
and if one was lucky
like the young daughter of Arsenia
who danced at night clubs
and escorted for the tourists,
there would be enough of what's needed.

Their daughters had grown up
lovely beauties of the slums.
The first got married early
and the second ran off
with a basketball player.
Only the youngest stayed
selling cigarettes and chewing gums
while Rufo and Myrna
continued to peddle smoked fish
in the city sidewalks.

Fishing in a Sapyaw

Brown muscles strained
as the fishermen pulled the net
heavy with the night catch.
Blazing lights played on the dark waters
like hundreds of fallen stars
dancing and swaying in the waves.

For fourteen nights without the moon
the fishermen watched for
phosphorescent signals confirming
the presence of fish, attracted
by the lights, underneath the waves.
All hands grabbed the net
hauled it up in harmony
with ancient melodies sung
by generations of fishermen.

Steady hands tugged hard
in rhythmic precision of the tides
heaving in the dark unsteady sea.
The net surfaced like an altar offering
of dashing, jumping and flapping fish
churning the inky water
as the men continued to sing
ancient melodies sung
by other fishermen before them.

Bloody Spectacle

He did not know how it happened
nor where the punch came from.
It was lightning fast, a flurry of punches
then a left-right combination to the head
before a left cross came crashing to the jaw.
The last conscious moment
he remembered was falling down
the canvass slowly, as in a dream,
amid the cheers and jeers of the crowd.

On the locker room he sat alone.
Pain was in his eyes.
There is no honor to gain
nor glory to chase.
Boxing is a bloody spectacle,
just like bullfight and cockfight,
that entertains the paying crowd.
It has been so through the ages
from the gladiatorial combat,
to the heavyweight bouts.
The more violent and brutal
the more entertaining.
The sight of blood and suffering,
excite the crowd who crave for more
as long as they are not the ones
who suffer.

The Tricycle Drivers of Catbalogan

Very early in the morning
the tricycle drivers of Catbalogan
pedal through the muddy streets
squeezing antique horns.
This is the sound that awakens
this coastal town from the comfort of sleep,
hundreds of honking horns.
The all too familiar sounds
reverberate along beaten pathways
setting the faithful rhythm
of daily life.

Their days follow fixed routine:
taking the kids to school
loading products at the pier,
taking employees to their offices,
moving people around
and bringing home those
who have been away.

In the darkened cubicles
which are their homes
they carefully count
the day's earnings
in the palms of their hands.

Setting aside the hiring fee
what is left is just enough
to survive for the next day
of pedaling through the streets
of Catbalogan
squeezing ancient horns.

I. G. Buenaseda

Baptism

She stood transfixed beside the bed
with a far away look in her eyes.
Framed in the open window
she was beautiful in her nakedness.
She could still feel the warm squirt
of blood on her arm, her baptism,
wherein she felt reborn and clean again.

Before her the landlord lay dying
with eyes of a frightened mouse.
He was clutching his breast
right where she pulled the blade
that impaled his heart.

She planned this for many nights
until she found the courage.
For years he crawled into her room
like a snake in the night
devouring her beauty
amid threats and promises.

The blood was still fresh in her hand
when she walked out
of the landlord's mansion,
her hair flapping loosely in the breeze
while in the distance
she could hear the siren wail.

Johnny

Each morning Johnny comes out
of the apartment ready to strike
at anyone who crosses his way.
There is fire in his eyes
obscene words cascade from his tongue
it is the way he relates to the world.

In school he is not doing well
although the teachers said he is bright
smart is a better word.
At most, he is a case study on behavior.
Neighbors predicted that he would
be in prison at an early age.

What have we done with our children
deprived of childhood innocence
in their tender years
immersed in the messy world
of adult impurities and fears?
The children have tv in their rooms
anyway, and a lot of electronic games.
They watch cartoons all day
secured in the solitude of their rooms
when they should have been playing
with other kids, learning to interact,
to take turns and respect other's feelings;
to run in the open, with the wind on their hair
and the soft touch of the rain on their faces.

But no, Johnny has no time for tenderness,
sympathy for him is an insult.
He was born with the unresolved
problems of his parents.
Johnny will continue to lash at the world
his defiance is an honest effort
·to destroy the structure that shaped him
and redeem his dignity from the ruins.

Lost Love

Memories come stealthily
on unguarded moments,
the private hours,
when sleep hesitates
on the threshold
of consciousness.

Why should I flay myself
with the thought of a lost love?
The past is final
stored away in memories
like a half-remembered song.

In this city of many faces
love could have lasted
if we had no other choice.
I could have returned
to rekindle old flames
but love once lost
is never regained.

I. G. Buenaseda

San Fermin

The sad resonance
of the churchbells
rippled through the
silent air of San Fermin.
It was the funeral march
for Manuel and Esteban.
They were planting watermelons
along the dried gullies
when the soldiers came
and took them away
at gunpoint.

Their wives and relatives
made daily search
but nobody could tell
their whereabouts.
There were no records
of their arrest and detention.

After a week their bodies
were found among the
water lilies of the lake..
their fingernails torn off,
Their bodies pockmarked
with cigarette burns.

The sound of the church bells
faded softly into the evening air
as the people buried their dead.
That night the men and women
of San Fermin did not sleep.
They sensed trouble more terrifying
than the long drought or the locusts.

At dawn,
the sonorous peals of the church bells
floated through the morning mist.
But San Fermin was an empty
cluster of huts and hovels,
desolate and abandoned.

I. G. Buenaseda

Banyan Trees of San Joaquin

People say it was the haunt
of the spirits, the banyan trees
lining the pathways to San Joaquin.
At night, mournful sounds
ooze among the thick foliage,
wails of lamentation
from the tree canopies.
For generations the pathways
were the undisturbed haunts
of the spirits.

Life became hard
for the people of San Joaquin
long dry seasons and the plague
visited upon them.
Strangely, the spirits and the mysteries
of the banyan trees disappeared.
What was left was the cool
and tranquil air of the pathways.
But the peace did not last long.
Soon the place became the haunts
of bandits and evil men
who robbed and terrorized
strangers and travelers.
The pathways became weird
and desolate once more.

Things changed only
when the guerillas came
with their unselfish love
for the people.
They drove away the bandits
and kept the pathways redolent
with the smell of honey
and champaca.

I. G. Buenaseda

Islands of Our Dreams

From a distance
they are tiny specks
rising in the mist,
dark and indistinct
in the twilight.
These are the islands
of our dreams
caressed by the sun
and nurtured by the sea.

The evening breathes softly,
ushering the shadows
and the monotonous lullabies
of the waves
evoking memories
extant only in the bosoms
of the islands.

Tomorrow,
these islands will awaken
to the long and lingering
sound of the fishermen's conches.
The sea provides the resources
while the islanders follow
the requirements of their lives
that remained unchanged
for generations.

Burning Words

I shall slay you
with my poems
pierce your heart
with burning words
and let the images
explode before your eyes
so that before dying
you may understand
the patience and courage
of our people.

To Evelyn

The plains are desolate now
the houses are deserted
the fields are left unattended
even the sparrows are gone.
No breeze rustle the leaves
and the silence is complete.

The peasants have gone
to pay their respect
to their martyr, Evelyn.
She could have been a teacher now
enjoying a normal life
with a family of her own.
But her heart lies beyond
the ordinary classrooms
wider than the boundaries
we set as limits to our
efforts and sacrifices.
She found higher fulfillment
in the service of the people
among the peasants of Nueva Ecija.

Evelyn is not totally gone
in death, she is transformed
into a symbol of our struggle.
She is our guiding star
constantly encouraging us
to overcome our
uncertainties and fears,
urging us to take unfamiliar paths,

learn from our mistakes,
and look at things and events
in their interrelation.
She taught us to rely
on the creative potentials of the masses
because being poor
they learned to handle everything
with patience and determination.
Evelyn has become a part of us
in our daily struggle in the green fields,
in sweatshops and in the academe

I. G. Buenaseda

The Old Man Fishing in the Coral Reef

The old man dropped his line and waited.
His fingertips could feel
the vibrations underneath the swell.
He kept jerking his line on little bites
which could only be sand gobbies
or a parrot fish nibbling at his bait.

He retrieved his line to check his bait
"Those little creatures down there
are stealing my bait" he mumbled to himself.
He lowered his line once more
with a fresh bait and patiently waited for a bite.
For ten minutes there was not a tug
or a nibble at the end of the line.
"Come on," he said, "a sand bass
or a grouper will be fine.
Come bonito, come skipjack,
give me just a bite."

Suddenly, a tug—heavy and firm.
it could not be a grouper nor a popper
groupers do not give a fight
this one was going around the boat
it could not be a bonito either
it was way down the bottom
although it had the same strength.

"This is a strange fish," the old man said.
He pulled on the taut line slowly at first
as the fish continued to dash and dive.
He looked down into the water
in childlike anticipation
searching for movement or a blur
as he retrieved the line.
He could feel the fish
Struggling to get free.
When it was about to reach
the visible part of the water,
the line lightened.
The old man quickly retrieved his line
and found out he had nothing
but a broken hook!

Slowly, the old man rowed back to shore
wondering what kind of fish
could cut a steel hook in two.

I. G. Buenaseda

Lonely Road

The way from LA to El Centro
is the long and desolate road
running endlessly across the desert.
It is the loneliness of an abandoned
fuel station buffeted by tumbleweeds.
On both sides of the road
are reminders of man's quest
for freedom and of his free spirit,
to roam the open space,
go after the receding horizons,
feel the unrestrained blowing of the wind
and sleep beneath the stars.

At times, one seems to hear
the desert whispering to the night.
They are only the residual impulses
of forgotten romances
that ran out of passion
mercilessly discarded from memory.

Once in a while a mountain would
break the monotony of the landscape.
Sometimes an oasis, a green spot
in a vast expanse of emptiness,
would show up in the hazy distance
only to disappear, like a mirage
in the wastelands of our lives.

Hope

Each day at down
She walks towards the sea
Looking far into the horizon
Hoping to see a speck or a glint
Bobbing in the waves.

Her eyes are the mirrors of sadness
Reflecting grief
She keeps deep in her heart.

It has been like this
Since her husband went out far
Into the sea one night
Many moons ago,
And never came back.

The Sea is in Our Hearts

1

The only way
to reach our hearts
is through the sea.
It is our door.

The beaches are our arms
perpetually embracing the night.
The stars are our eyes
reflected on the dark water.

We are born of the waves
colliding with the rocks
suspended for glorious moments
before falling in million sprays
that gently merge with the tide
like the phosphorescent
fragments of a dream.

The temper of the sea
vibrates in our blood.
The breeze carries our songs
As we cage the tempest
In our hearts.

2

We are of the islands
brown by the sun,
blown by the wind.

In the twilight
the islands are indistinct
drenched in mist and memory,
mysterious and serene.

Other eyes saw the islands
from a distance,
so virginal in their beauty.
They heard our songs
the drumbeats of our hearts
echoing across the valleys.

They came with the monsoon
dragging their false gods
on the muddy fields
erasing images and memories
leaving skeletons on their wake.
They marched through our villages
trampled our rice fields
and blocked the sun.

The shadows spread wide
across the land.

"Do not be afraid,"
our ancestors said,
"flowers bloom naked
in the darkness."

For how long shall we
journey through these waters?
How many more horizons to chase
before we find the footprints
of our forebears?
Not a trace of our ancestors
remain in us.

Do not look at me for answers
the islands have their secrets
their strength and their charms.
They are faithful to the sea
constant and changeless
through the ages.

3

It is our martyrs,
even those who speak
with foreign tongues
who showed us the way
towards the sea, the sea
everything returns to the sea.

We carry in our consciousness
the collective experience of our people
their struggles and their dreams
distinct and typical of the islands
and the hidden valleys within.

We are young
and time is on our side.
It is in the sea
where we shall find
traces of our ancestors.
We shall find once more
the greatness, the elegance
and the honor of our race.
They are extant among
these islands in the mist,
in the intimate embrace of the sea.

I. G. Buenaseda

Falling Leaves

The leaves are falling
One by one
On the forest floor.
These are the days
That passed
Since we left the plain
The warmth of our homes
To scale with bare feet
Hidden mountain paths
Cross silent rivers
And seek shelter
Among the shadows
Of the mountainside.

We crisscrossed the terrain
Until we became parts
Of the rocks and the shades
Until we blend with
The draperies of leaves
Learned to stay motionless
Like some reptile
Poised to recoil in ambush
Or to submerge for hours
In the unforgiving swamps
For it is here
In the heart of the forest
Where we lure and ensnare
The enemy.

The leaves continue to fall
One by one
On the forest floor.

Light from the Heart

Deep in my heart
I lighted a candle.
Its soft light and small flame
Like a firefly
Small and alone in the dark.
The light radiated
Ripples of compassion
Growing bigger and wider
In a series of shining rings
Pushing the darkness away.

They Shoot Simple Peasants

The old women,
Their faces behind black viels,
Came solemnly
To claim the body
Of Francisco
Who at the age of twenty
Have not gone to school
And stutters when he talks
But always ready to help
In preparing the fields,
In transplanting
And in other tasks
He could share with the people.
He was a simple peasant.

Francisco was shot down
At high noon
In the cornfields
When armed men ordered
Him to stop.
Confused and afraid at the sight
Of guns and strange men
Francisco opted to run.

And they shot him
Shot him like a wild pig
At high noon
Among the maturing corns.

Class Reunion

The excitement was high
almost electric.
Seeing each other
after forty years!
The familiar sights in the campus:
the tiled corridors
the old auditorium
with the stillness of its empty seats
so silent, almost brooding.
The trees in the campus
have grown so big.
The curved hearts and
arrows were still in their trunks.

"You have not changed much
after all these years, Helen.
You too, Melchor. You were the
one who made us laugh.
And you, Clemente,
you led us on protest marches
against the dictatorship
or anything we believed
to be unjust and inhuman.
We thought you joined
the rebels in the hills.
Have you heard of Rodolfo,
our class president?
He migrated to the US
and became a school principal.
Some of our classmates

went abroad too: Emma, Fe,
Norma, Beatrice and Lucia.
They are now domestic helpers
in Hong Kong and Italy.
Remember Patricio, the silent guy?
He made it good in the south
married to a rich landowner
in Davao where he raised
fighting cocks.
And how about Evelyn
the editor from our class?
Evelyn won't be with us today.
You know she and her husband
were active in the mass movement.
They went underground
when martial law was declared.
We learned that she died
in an encounter
with the military
in the plains of Nueva Ecija."

We went our separate ways
Right from graduation
and after forty years
we have our lives to share.

The Survivor

I saw what happened.
They came at dawn
Those men in black
So sudden they were
All over the village
They rounded up everybody
The way they always do
Those men in black.
I saw the worried look
On my mother's eyes
As she drew my younger brother
Closer to her breast.
She knew that I had escaped.

Those men in black
With arrogant visage
And disdainful eyes
Had been here before.
They told us to move out
And settle somewhere else
The village of Sag-ud is within
The lumber concession
Of their employer.

The precise bursts
Of gunfire ripped through
The tranquil air of dawn.
Outstretched fingers claw
At empty space
Terror flashed on the faces

Of those who fell.
Those who tried to escape
Were gunned down as they ran
Nobody was left alive.
They didn't leave witnesses
Those men in black.

I saw what happened in Sag-ud
I memorized their faces
And I am going back someday.

I. G. Buenaseda

Ms Johnson at the Eve of Her Retirement

Ms Johnson has been teaching
for thirty long years
and retiring this year
to enjoy the fruits
of patience and dedication.

This morning
her first grade student
told her to fuck off.

The incident shocked her
not because of the language
but by the vehemence in which
the child delivered those words.

Ms Johnson knew
the child was trying to
communicate something
deeper than the nasty words.
He screamed at her.
She looked into the eyes
of the child with compassion
the way she always did.
There was no trace of innocence
that should be in every child.
There was only a hidden sadness
Filmed by defiance and hate.

With lonesome eyes
Ms Johnson remembered
the names and the faces
of those who passed
by her classroom through the years.
Some of them are parents
of those she is teaching now
each have gone their own ways
lost in the busy maze
of crisis and deadlines
taking their shares of the joys
and tragedies of this world.

"Have I influenced their lives?
Have I been a part of their growth
their personalities and what they are now?
Do they remember me from time to time?"
And she realized that all these times
names and faces she could no longer recall
have left her classroom as she welcomed
those who came after them in a continuing
circle through the years.
Ms Johnson wished they remember her
even for just a moment
at the eave of her retirement.

I. G. Buenaseda

About the Author

Igmedio G. Buenaseda was born and studied in the Philippines. He started writing poetry at an early age. His works appeared in such publications as *Midweek, Focus, Graphics, The Insomniac, The Lyceum and The Torch*. Buenaseda is personally familiar with the specter of oppression, having been active in the anti-dictatorship movements. He believes that poetry is not merely a creative expression faithful to its forms and rhythm. It must assume a militant character, which is responsive to the issues and problems of the time. Buenaseda is currently teaching adult classes at the Manual Arts Community Adult School in Los Angeles.

9 781403 328489